T0088895

Other Books By Zoë Flowers

From Ashes to Angel's Dust: A Journey
Through Womanhood 2016

Five Reasons You're Stuck 2019

In Praise of The Wytch

Zoë Flowers

BALBOA.PRESS
A DIVISION OF HAY HOUSE

Balboa Press books may be ordered through booksellers or by contacting:

Balboa Press
A Division of Hay House
1663 Liberty Drive
Bloomington, IN 47403
www.balboapress.com
844-682-1282

Print information available on the last page.

ISBN: 978-1-9822-6185-6 (sc)
ISBN: 978-1-9822-6186-3 (e)

Balboa Press rev. date: 02/03/2021

Dedicated to the awkward silences.

Contents

A WOMAN CAN BE
A PRISONER
A PRINCESS
OR
HERSELF

CHINESE PROVERB

Introduction

In Praise of The Wytch is a collection of musings about things unsaid, race relations, gender, unreliable sources, misadventures in love, and reflections on the modern world.

Spirit Guide Message received December 2015
*Speaking your truth gives others the
confidence to do the same.*

We Back Girlz 3-based on a true story

A soft place to land a place without critique a place with
soft eyes and no work no landmines emotional
a soft place to lay wooly head
cotton soft
a place with arms strong enough to hold the weight of this
black girl experience
where is this place
we die looking for this place
We die looking for it in angry men's beds and the arms of
mothers who wasn't loved proper
we die looking for it in hateful sista circles
we die trying to be seen and heard and believed we die
trying to rebirth still born adults
Using our good air on the undeserving
We stay dying trying to be reborn in orgasm and
organizations
A million indignities from womb to tomb
we get off hospital gurney if we make it
and come home not to self but to dishes unclean like we
A million indignities
We come home if we make it to groceries that need cooking
and trash to be taken out like we
we come home to ourselves less and less
Dodging think pieces about how we should best react to
our trauma
Did she say trauma?
Black girl trauma
Is she still talking out that?
Best to not speak about your trauma sista
Best to keep your fucking mouth shut
stay pleasant and feminine

What about the people in Guatemala sista? You don't have it so bad over here.
Best to keep your mouth shut and suffer silently
You're more attractive that way
Your rage is not feminine or needed
Unless you're fighting for not you
Then your mouth should be open wide outstretched receiving mode
On the front lines
Then you can speak sista
Then we will hear you sista
Your voice is necessary sista
What about them poor folks in Africa?
What about da brothas' sista?
Your worries no..... stay quiet bout dat sista
Dying in childbirth no no no no no sista
Women die all over the world sista
You say they treated you like shit from dust to dawn
No sista it's about prison reform right now
See there's people out there really suffering you're just being selfish again sista
It's not about your life
You got to get out and get people to vote sista
That's the vibe right now sista
Lives is on the line right now sista
We'll get to yours later
We promise

Sincerely,
The World

The Married Man

And he says, "why'd you call"
And she says
"I don't know"
he says,
"It's been a long time
The Silence"

Surely longer for her than him
Long days of self-denial
And reprisals
Of using common sense
talking herself out of making calls and texts
many moons of tossing and turning in beds empty

Cocky in her self-discipline
Steadfastly strong
As she carefully constructs her walls
And yeah
it *has* been long
6 months of keeping Him at bay lest she fall prey
to the slickness of his ways at arm's length
they stay

But today
They meet
She steadies herself
And remembers how tapeworm skinny
she feels after his retreat
He reminds her of her father all sunshine
and promise until he leaves

He says she's good to see
And that he regrets nothing
She thinks to herself - why would he
Asking again why she called
She says new moon in cancer
fogs her thinking and decimates resolve
Making her forget all that she should recall

He recites her poetry
She smiles
He goes on
He tells her she's beautiful
She feels a slight crack in her walls
She steals herself
Remembering-his flattery isn't anything much at all
She remembers his flattery is nothing
more than a tool of the cunning
And like sex it can be traded
For much like sex, his flattery too is a commodity

To the Boy That Liked Boys

Sanitized flowers
Decorate perfect mirrors
In your house
A house
I could
get used to
Put my feet up
And
Stretch into
Underneath
Make a part of me
If invited

The Rebound

We lay quiet
In Brooklyn
Where the love resides
Snow cocoons the city
Transforms
Forced stillness
At last
Shut in
We stir
Trapped
Alone
Together
While Mother Nature
Has her say

No Cap

I wanna feel you Wanna be all up in your
business Let my mouth wander
surrender
to demands
I wanna take you Wanna wake up
and know your there

smell you
on pillowcase

I wanna snatch you away from
possessions

keep you
under lock and key

Eat dance make love spoon fight
drank

on the first date

I want you

bound
gagged
tied down
low
submissive

I wanna see you Show Me
Everything

the funky
black bottom
broke down
callous
controlling
side

                    I ain't scared I am well versed in
bar room brawl
back alley interlude
and
gutter punk
                    I wanna savor you on tongue like
                    Alaga on corn cake
                    So come home so I can

Scorpio Season

Your gaze
Pierced
My soul
and I
was struck dumb
Rendered numb
Like a deer
frozen
in headlights

The Bronx Apartment

We sit
Waiting for the mood to change
Our hearts heavy with things un-said
We sit
Quiet
Words wouldonlymakethismomentmovefaster
And I
Want to stop time
Want to
Hold it in my palms
Like a captured butterfly
Swallow it whole
Wings beating against my cheeks
Then let it sit
In the pit
Of my stomach
Till I can birth beautiful
From this silence

Dat Scorpio..again

*We keep
pain buried *
deep in bones *
dry and brittle *
We break*
apart*easy

Gemini Season

Nighttime is the worst
Nigh time is the worst time because
Nigh time is the worst time because I can't
Nigh time is the worst time because I can't run
Nigh time is the worst time because I can't run from the
memory of your lips parting mine
Nigh time is the worst time because I can't run from the
memory of your lips parting mine using tongues wet hands
gripping hips arched backs

Nigh time is the worst time because I can't disappear
myself away from loving you
Daytime is so much nicer
In darkness it's hardest to divest from memories of folding
into flesh
They say there are 7 layers in the human auric field
Each one with its own existence its own reality that we visit
in our dreams
If that's true, then that means
That right now there is some place where there is still a me
and you
And if that's true then that's where I'm moving to
Cause whatever plane our love exists in that's the one I
need to live in
cause this one only reminds me
that were broken
That you're gone and I'm forgotten

I want to take back the night from you and reclaim my sleep
Rally myself around the idea of some kind of peace
Start a movement like women did in the 70's to take back
the streets
But there's no support groups for bad decisions
Ain't no vigils being held for heartache
No organizations for women who bypassed red flags when
something told them to pump the brakes

Wanna to take back my nights, but you own them
Taking up too much space like hipsters in Brooklyn you
spreading
Getting too fucking comfortable like gentrification
I try to stop you but like Harlem landlords you stay winning
Circling my slumber like vultures over carrion
Daring my sleep to say something like New York pigeons
I swear my memories be like "oh. she's healing?" dis the
perfect time to get it in
DJ bring that beat back
Anna Karenina was probably just sleepy when she laid on
them tracks
Cause love will haunt you
It's crazy even if you deaded it you're the one that feels
like a fool
Night dreams of wet dreams have you trippin' like maybe
I ended it too soon
Maybe I was the one that was lazy lack of sleep due to lack
of love will have reality looking real hazy
have you hitting up psychics like Swayze
It's crazy
Even when you the one to end it you feel like the fool
Night dreams of wet dreams
Have you trippin' like maybe I left him too soon

But that's just night talk
Cause in the daylight I can see you
You can haunt me all you want
I will never call you
I can do this shit all night
I can do this shit with my eyes closed

On Easter Sunday

As I look at you
As I listen to you speak
As I watch you brush your teeth
Eat breakfast
I am realizing
You are only part human
As I look at you
Watch you dress
Listen to you lecture me
About what to do with my body
I see now you are
A walking breathing idiot who is kind of
no definitely
a dick
different than a penis -a dick is borderline unbearable -unless
it's nighttime late like 3am
The Wytches hour
Then a dick a real one
can be quite
Useful
And maybe that's how I let myself
Get caught
But Today
On Easter morning
With the sun shining on you-direct
As I see you looking through me again
I realize
You are most definitely the wrong kind of dick

WHY I left

My vibe is circular - has a life of its own - is fond of tight clothes and toe paint... loud

My vibe is circular - has a life of its own - is fond of tight clothes and lip paint... purple

My vibe is circular - has a life of its own - is fond of tight clothes and men funky with the call of the wild so strong it clings

My vibe is circular - has a life of its own - is fond of tight clothes and strong arms...unless strong-armed

My vibe is circular - has a life of its own – is not fond of your brand -it judges, measure mistakes, leaves a mark

To be frank..Frank
your vibe

is
choking
my
vibe
out

Dat Lanky Yellow Boy

Did you know as you slept I watched
Your mouth
twitch
Your eyes
flutter

savoring your every maneuver
As if preparing for your
departure

Leo Season

I made you my muse fo I knew who you was
I could write you poems in perfect iambic
pentameter every single day
and it wouldn't change NOthing
so I'm gone stop writing you

I could strip naked fall on floor and let you take me
every single hour and you'd still......

so

I'm gone stop laying with you

I exist in the cracks left by projects and other
conquests

so

I'm gone stop existing for you

I could tell you bout' energetic cords strengthened
by our lovemaking
but you ain't here to hear

so

I'm gone loose myself and go

The One That Pleased Himself

We lay
a hare's breath between us
The distance
wide
Steady
cavernous
And yet
when flesh presses into mine
I believe
Tonight, will be different
i dive deep
Splash round
emersed
Water fills nostrils
so close to drowning
So far from shore
so far
Too
quick
You
pluck me out
Return to land
leave me floating
to shore dry

Scorpio

I recall
Eyes
Distant and longing
For something
Untouchable
By
Me
Nothing has changed

Libra Season

You think
She's sweet
A breath of fresh air
For your arid lungs
Is all that you see
You inhale
Deep

You love how she still believes
Despite those who say the odds are against her
She
Black woman
With opinions
Anticipating a love
She can
Shout about
Can sing
Like a hymn
A love she can
Wear to church-and stomp to
A love
That will
Fill her
Holy Ghost like
So deep she can
Swim in
Be drenched in
Stretched into
And
Worn to bed
Like a lover's t-shirt

A love that
Understands
And encourages
And believes in revolution
And loves its people- loves its people- loves its people
And ... loves... her

The End of Leo Season

I stood with you in the garden.
Waiting for the dust to settle
After the beating - the first one emotional
We gathered
picked up pieces
Put bow in hair
And presented ourselves as new
As if unbroken, uncracked
As if whole still
The second encounter
Found us turning away from exit signs
Looking for validation where no one lived
I show up as whisper
Starve myself thin
Make myself small enough to fit under his boot

I stood with you in the garden.
We were surrounded by the dead.
The locusts were the only things that lived. I shuddered.
You held my hand.
I told myself. This is love.
Show me the exact place where I ceased to exist.
Was it the last time we fucked?
When you whispered,
"I'm sorry" so softly I could barely hear it.
Was it then?
Were you apologizing in advance e for disappearing me?
Retracing my last steps like a missed period
I search the city for my corpse or at least some fucking
police tape.
I mean. Why was there no funeral?
Why did no one tell me I was dead?

Gone to Soon

When someone dies and it's not you
you thank god that your settlement
was passed over this time
scourge avoided
And you are left intact
When someone dies and it's not you
you feel lucky
if you're a poet who can wrap
yourself in words and isolate
When someone dies and it's not you
you walk slower for about a week
get up late
tell people you love them
and fuck better than you have in a really long time
When someone dies and it's not you
you pay attention to cracks on street
watch lovers intently
and hold your children closer until
they begin to bore you again
When someone dies and it's not you
you stop complaining and even smile
at strangers for like three days
When someone dies and it not you keeping dr.'s
appointments become very very important
When someone dies and it's not you
you make plans for how you'll be better,
kinder and take less for granted
until you forget

Spirit Guide Message received December 2015
When you ask for enlargement, you're asking the Universe to enlarge your reach influence but also your compassion, understanding, lives etc. You must also understand anything being birthed comes with a certain amount of pain. Pain is a sign that new life is on the way!!!

The Body Politic

Our bodies are
Snatched
Pinched
Cinched
We be porn star Thin
Shaved bald
And quietly itching

Our bodies stay
Snatched
Cinched
Pinched
We are addicts
Chomping at Kardashian bits
our lives defined by likes and clicks

With bodies
Snatched
Pinched
Whipped
We are submissives
Sculpted to the point of dismembering
Constantly measuring
comparing
and repairing

These bodies stay
Snatched
Pinched
Stitched
Flaws sewn in
Asses packed tight like clubs
so exclusive
Our spirits need reservations

Persons of Interest

Calvin Wise & Laura Green
Her, stout 46 years of age
Him, well-built 5'11, 198 lbs.
The place Philadelphia
The year 1963
The crimes loitering gambling breathing while black
Not enough to be arrested for actually doing nothing
Not enough to be hauled in for trying to
put a little money in his pocket
Not enough to be locked up for loitering
gambling breathing while black
No insult is added to injury
Misdeeds published for the public to see
Laura her hair looking like who did it and ran
after, like she intended to be out for a second, like
she rolled outta bed realized she needed bread
and ran out the house like what the fuck
Calvin looking confused like the rent was due
and he was short, so he went on down to the
local spot to test his luck and now he's stuck
Their trials are more reminiscent of an auction block
If they could have, they would have shown us more
If it was 1803
They'd have spread her open
Shown us his dick
But since they couldn't legally
They locked them up legally
Criminalized
Institutionalized
Always on display
Calvin Wise & Laura Green

Her stout 46 years of age
Him well built 5'11, 198
pounds
Immortalized for the rest of their days
If they could have, they would have shown us more
Than the peculiar pain reserved for Black women
screaming through her eyes and jumping off the page
Calvin still looking dazed
Criminalized
Institutionalized
1963 1993 2003 2016
Not enough to be killed for wearing a hoodie
Not enough to be killed during a stop and frisk
No insult is added to injury
When even after your murdered you
are portrayed as the risk
Always on display
But beautifully invisible
Their suffering is so inspiring
Blacks make gorgeous ghosts don't they
Perfect hangers for judgment
Blank slates for all manner predilection and fantasy
1703 1783 1803 1893 1903 1963 1983 1993 2003 2020
What's been done to them would be criminal
If they were human

This is Gonna Leave A Mark

How many rocking in corners wondering why
How many uncomfortable moments at water cooler
How many times on bended knee?
How many bitten lips endured
How many boycotts?
How many ain't nobody got time for boycotts
How many ancestors turning over in graves?
How many you fit the description of
How many stop or I'll shoot
How many shot without warning
How many he just went around the corner
How many
stop playing the "race card"
I didn't own slaves
you can't blame me
that's reverse racism
How many vigils
How many acquittals
How many
"this will be the last time – I promise"
"there's no such thing as rape culture"
isolated incidents
we don't have all the facts
there's two sides to every story
she must like the abuse
if that was me I woulda left
it takes two to tango
why didn't she just leave
How many she went to his house to break it off for good
How many songs sung, poems written, expletives flung
across the page?

How many artists, poets, dancers, dead with their music still in them

How many artists, poets, dancers, healers not getting paid

How many insults added to injury by naming streets, and cities and towns and sports teams after people you tried to wipe off the page

How many my culture is not a costume?

How many sacred circles?

Histories erased by educated fools

How many followed around stores based on appearance

How many "we treat everyone the same" before they kill you for your gender expression

How many what makes you think you own your body features scorned unless on a lighter hue

How many looking in mirrors hating their reflection

How many skin lighteners liposuctions breast implants

How many I am not good enoughs'

How many you're right you're not good enough

How many "this is the greatest country in the world" before they shoot you

How many "we don't see color" before they tie you to the back of a truck

How many "that was a long time ago" before they call you a black bitch on a song or a nigger at a comedy club

How many "guns don't kill people" before they march into a school and kill your children

How many No Justice No Peace while we stay peaceful?

It's Game...Baby

Is a movement really a movement or something else when
Its members sit idly by watching families fall apart,
staff being abused, poor decisions being made,
cover ups, and people getting sicker and sicker?

Is a movement really a movement or something else when
Leaders say nothing and watch its members work
too much, drink too much, eat too much, and smile
too little?

Is a movement really a movement or something else when
What is said matters more than what is done?

Is a movement really a movement or something else when
Once you're gone, you're forgotten-disposable
and erased when no longer useful?

Is a movement really a movement or something else when
Its members are valuable only as long as they can
keep their crazy, pain, and trauma to themselves

Is a movement really a movement or something else when
Its better to be superhuman or better yet non-
human for the cause

Gentrified Soul

They ain't no good
Got no soul
Their stories full of holes
But we still buy it
They got no hearts
They is full of shit
Got the whole world thinking they important
But we know we not
Spend our time fucking away memories of auction blocks
and the gnawing feeling that we coming up short
Exploiting the short cuts
We got no pride
only Trust in what we indulge in
Sex is our language
Cause we commitment phobic
We be hustlers
Breaking all promises
Don't expect us to feel
Cause we be zombie
And you are walking dead like us
You mean nothing
You are nothing
You are no thing
You are not things
You are
You

Rules for The Talented Tenth

Nothing exists in a vacuum
Nothing but empty caverns holding space for regret
Nothing but bone-dry deserts and cracked lip wastelands
Nothing but broke leg swimmers choking on polluted waters

Nothing exists in a vacuum
You didn't get here by yourself
You owe
See you need to know
We don't do burping's, bibs or baby clothes bought in bargain basements
We got no time for surprises in diapers, throw up on shoulders or pee squirted into faces
No late-night feedings
No clandestine pumps of liquid gold
No stretch marks, stretched out vaginas or outstretched arms from highchairs
No saggy titties from too much sucking
We stay tight

Maybe you seen pictures of us??
Please don't hate us cause were beautiful!
Smiling back at you in snapshots from family vacations or posted up next to Cadillac's, Lincoln's, and Coups

We don't do Mocha moms or La Leche clubs or eyes that light up when we walk into rooms
We be too fly for minivans

You might a read about us in a book or something,

we believe in family values,
We got no time for prenatal vitamins mocking us from medicine cabinets or I can't believe I'm in this clinic again expressions

We be those I left Augusta when I was 17 to make a betta life,
how's it gonna look you bringing babies in this house outta wedlock, yes, I belong to the masons and eastern star,
up standing, upper middle class black folk
who still shoot craps in back allies,
buy TV's from boosters
and play numbers outta dream books kept on nightstands
we be good stock

We're those we're better cause we just are kinda' folk
With a tradition of raising daughters and loving sons, women who cooks they asses off but still have plenty to spare and men who work hard and play harder we got that new car every year, high expectations lineage

We be too fabulous for untimely 1st 2nd & 3rd trimesters
Unsprouted seeds are better served sitting stacked on beauty counter shelves

We be them I don't understand you Black Americans,
I left Jamaica when I was 10,
please don't call me African,
those dreadlocks are not attractive, kinda kin
Maybe you heard a us,
we be that 1st black family in the neighborhood,
1st black family on the block that works for self and buys instead of rents

memories of downturned eyes, gray carpet, and cold feet in stirrups are left un-remembered

Maybe you know about us
We dat Jamaican Rum and Johnny Walker Red before breakfast and bedtime family
With them good men, some of them even got that good hair,
You know the ones who pay all the bills
And hand paychecks over to women who love men who love other women, pull yourself up from your bootstraps set

This family has rules
Look at no one when entering or leaving the clinic
Tell no one
And have good insurance so you can sleep through it

Bottle Battle

You have a relationship you have relations and I can't be mad cause y'all been together way befo me but I'm here now and I'm asking you to recognize that you're different that it changes you that you ain't the same as you used to
Be
So
We can't be the same You can't expect me to play second fiddle to pretend that I understand the riddle that plagues us three
I mean you say you love me but when I say what I see you shut me down or just leave
Gone off to that other place you be That place untouchable by me and no matter how much I beg
You
Don't
See
Cause ya'll got a relationship ya'll got relations and as much as I hate it ya'll been kicking it way befoe' me So it don't even matter if that bottle leaves you battered it's your company when I leave it's always within reach it's silent and consistent it's company I get it you put time in studying bottoms of empty glasses
Who
Am
I to even comment Still I make measure of the levels I can't help it - I scope your movements holding breath until your eyes shift Then the mood tips, I watch the levels get lower and lower and lower as the vowels get slower and slower
And it's so sad to see
But
ya'll got a relationship ya'll got relations and as much as I hate it ya'll been kicking it way befoe' me

FORCED MARRIAGE
CIRCA 1619

Wrapped up wrapped up wrapped
up in memory in the silence
in the distance
that's you
that's me and I can't breathe
I can't see
I Don't see Anything
'Cept you
In memory
Memorieeees lie and die over and over and over in this life
and I can't breathe You only see what U wanna see
that's you
That's me
but it's not even a memory
It's reality
Wish I knew how to leave
Wish I knew how to be
I did this I do this I did it I did it
You did this you do this you did it you did it
I got a million fucking reasons I should leave you
but I don't I won't
this is life this is war this is us
till death
Do US

Red, White, & Blue

Black, and bruised again and again
Silenced shut down pushed down pulled down we bounce

Red, white, blue, Black, and bruised
Silenced shut down pushed down pulled under
we bounce
back
are buoyant

Red, white, blue, Black, and bruised we bounce back
Buoyant
float
Up
From Silence
This time
Always
Carrying songs
and
Medicine
and
Poetry

Red, white, blue, Black, and bruised we rise and gather
become
medicine
and
music
and
poetry
we emerge
carrying
the whole world on our backs

Gone to Soon 2

We gathered
in that funky hospital room with the old white lady on the other bed throwing up, shitting, and crying for her daughter Meagan

Meagan was nowhere to be found
It was just us four black women your sisters watching your breathing and counting

We stood, sat, hovered, rested, and were startled awake

"Wait! Did you see her twitch when we turned on Miles Davis? Turn the music up!"

We railed against the medical industrial complex and seethed as bored nurses took your vitals and shuffled you our sister around like cotton

we sat there watching you to die
You fully expected to live to 100
2 days ago, you were making plans for your garden 5 hours ago, you complimented my style and now "I think her skin is getting Warmer! Do you feel it? Rub her harder!" Fucking cancer Even your doctor was in disbelief
For six hours I sat there convinced my magick could will you back to life until I realized I was wrong

Privilege

Ice cream truck whizzing by
Golf clubs hit their mark
This is the good life

Normal
They said it was a problem with his head

His didn't function like ours
special ed
special classes
tests
inconclusive
still
every day is more beautiful than the last
and then
the blast

Normal
They said it was a problem with his head

In pictures he stuck out
You could see it
he was different
and everybody knew it

Normal
They said it was a problem with his head

the family kept to itself
played war games
shopped for rifles

rite of passage
but it was no one's fault

Normal
They said it was a problem with his head

we did the best we could
surrounded him by the best the brightest the lightest
raised him up right
brought him up white

Normal
They said it was a problem with his head

that day he had the power
hard black and familiar
the rife felt good in his hands
like so many times before
but today it would be different

they say said it was a problem with my head
that confusion resides in the mind
but I know who I am
I grew in isolation
Blossomed under their noses
Stopped golf clubs stop mid swing
The rifle felt good in my hands
Hard black familiar
I was made for this
Cause they never see me coming

We Black Girlz 2

We write our pain on paper so it can live
Live
Live
We are liiiiivng
We are getting our whole lives
and when they see us
the people be like
Yaaas queens
There go the Black girlz
They be watching us
Live
And
Breathe
And fuck
so well
very well
very very well
it's so well Black girlz be like
oh well (shrug)
to everything
cause
It's lit
We lit
We are living
We are getting our whole lives
And when they see us
The people be like
Yaaas queens
Here come dem Black girlz
They be watching us
We be livid and living well-Still

We be still -and moving
We be confused
But biiiitch at least we living
we are living
we is living
we are livid /Make no mistake
but
Bitch
We make livid look lit
Black pain is enigmatic
Black girlz pain good
You pain good
You pain so good
You should get paid for it
I mean
you should
I mean
you deserve
but
you don't know It sooooooo
I'll take it
I
I mean
They'll take it
your heart, soul, brilliance, money, hair, lips, ass, titties,
spirit, stamina, talent, hopes, dreams and complexions
I
I mean
he she, they We, will take it
We will take all of you
And when they see us
The people gone be like
Yaaas queens

Here come everybody else
And you be watching us
Take everything you got
Everything you got
Except
Your pain
You can have that
I mean
That's yours
to Keep
Cause
Everybody knows Black girlz
Make pain
Look lit

Spirit Guide Message received December 2015
Instead of running from pain-love it. Use it as proof that new life new opportunity and new love is on the way.

I Apologize - A Monologue

I gave it up so quickly. I don't know... I
guess I didn't see the value of it
Didn't see it as a resource
Or whatever
I don't know I was.... so African about the whole
Traded... gave it away... really...if I'm truthful
And before I knew
Without checking
Without asking....
I wasn't prepared...the weaponry
Of it all
It's like the way we take advantage of the sun
You know it's always gonna be there
So, you don't think about it really ...am I making sense
I mean it's always there shining... even when it isn't
On some level... you just know...(sigh) you know
And that's how it was (beat)
I let the cold in
Opened the door wide and said
"Come on in.
No. Bring your selfishness too."
Why leave it outside all by itself?"
I tried to make him comfortable."
I Tempered ...shrunk myself low
So, I could... you know... fit ...easier...
in his pocket or whatever
I didn't even mind being tucked
behind the important things.
Strong women we long for...
I tried...and maybe he did too...
But it...it still...just... got all...fucked up.

45

I tempered the storms ...I thought I ... that he could ....
I thought he liked a challenge...
he's competitive ...you know
The sex? Generally, it was ...taken... like something
owed... like it wasn't even mine after a while. He needed
release ...he's busy... important... you know ..important
men need that ..no strings ..but when they're ready...
There comes a moment
A break
A split
Between, head, heart, and gut
between knowing and leaving surrender and the fight

There
Comes
A
Moment
When brokenness becomes too heavy
Rejection too close to bone
When the reflection is too damn crisp

I just got tired of feeling thrift store.
You know?
I just wanted to feel the sun again

Seasons Change. I have not.

It's spring
we're 11 days in
re-birthing
I leave again
just like last year
I leave for the last time
or at least
until
the fall

It's Hell. But I love it.

So, here I am
in my own head
wondering what I did
what I said
this time
what I didn't do
and didn't say
to make you stay
this time
I'd leave
but I'm committed to fighting for what isn't good
for me
I'm committed to suffering
I'd sew the gaping hole in my chest where my love lives
If I loved myself

The Cost

She discovered "the truth"
Innocently enough
Secondhand information
Taken as authentic
And since no one told her about accepting candy from strangers
She swallowed it
Whole
Letting the poison take over
"just a woman"
Knowledge that stifles
Creativity
And
Hope
And
Energy
Words that
Spread
Cancer like
Quickly
Starting at her feet traveling upward
Final destination
Her heart
Settling for a while in the pit of her stomach
Devouring her slowly
From the inside out
At times she sees traces of who she could be
In his eyes
Feels herself in his touch
And more than ever
She begins looking
For the rest herself in his shadow

My Karma

What does it mean when I feel rope round neck and lean closer to the tree
what does it mean when you've proven that your mean, unhealthy, abusive, illusive
married, attached, detached, inconsistent, distant, or just plain no good
for me
What does it mean when even then I seek your approval more than my self-esteem
that I keep falling flat backed failing waiting for your call
What does it mean that I spend holidays and birthdays and Saturdays and more sad than happy days looking out windows the same ways I did on
daddy never came days
Peering round corners hoping your shadow won't catch me slippin'
Hoping that Something about ME would make YOU be different
Wishing that I was good enough to capture your spirit
I'm a liar
Pretending I didn't know what I knew
Pretending it didn't matter that you didn't see me
Pretending that it was mutual that I didn't want more than what I got
That I gave it up too quickly and went from being intriguing to just an after thot
Pretending that I don't feel like that ho over there that got caught
Pretending the sex game is a mystery
When I know how the movie ends
I'm just another history lesson waiting to happen

I feel myself drifting to the outer banks of your memory
just another name on the list now
It's a waste of time asking why or what or how
I shoulda did that earlier
No, it's too late for that now
And we don't have time to talk about why or how cause
we're onto to the next phase of the game now
And you've moved on
And this is the part where I post sexy pics of myself on
social media just to remind you what you're missing before
I unfriend, unfollow and delete all your contact information
Except that one email with your number at the bottom
See now is the time where I spend hours
plotting about what I'll be wearing when I see you and I
already know what I'm gonna say to prove that I'm just as
heartless as you
See this is the part where I feign strength for girlfriends
who ask "what's up wid ole boy"
I am fully prepared to downplay the entire situation
I won't tell them
That
I'm not writing
Or that all I really want to do is sleep and sleep and sleep
cause that's the only place where I can still feel you
So, I just live there
As Much as possible
cause down here
I'm just another chick attracting same dude over and over
and over and over
while telling myself that I'm different

What we Know

1.
This longing is so familiar
that it's mistaken for real
Mistaken
For love
When thirsty
Living in dessert
Throat dry
Lips cracked open
It's easy
to mistake sweat
For rain shower
Easy to see
Rocks ordinarily stepped over
As diamond
Rough
Easy to misread
A man
Common
Mediocre
Regular
As Messiah

2.
Adorned in Sunday best
I arrive
Lay prostrate
Head bowed
Begging for sacrament

For light to shine on my face
I love in ways unimaginable
By him
Still

3.
My face betrays nothing
Actions controlled
Steps watched
Careful to avoid land mines
Confessions
Confrontation
Silently I storm
Stomach
tills frustration
Heart
Fertile ground for his indifference
Yielding crops of more longing
So familiar that it's mistaken for real

Never Forget

This is not how love behaves
Love doesn't call u when it wants something
It wakes you up at night just because
Thinks of you before itself

This is not how love feels
A good love fills your chest with air
Does not knock the wind out of you
Doesn't go MIA when you need it most
triggering memories of abandonment
Doesn't forget to call u when the game is on
This is not how love endures
A healthy love gives openly, honestly and always makes room
Love supports and upholds virtue
Sees the best in you
And wants the best for itself
Looks for possibilities
Open windows
Blue skies
And most importantly
Seeks that which like unto itself
Doesn't hog all the blankets, eat everything in the fridge without replacing it, doesn't return your car on empty, doesn't smoke in your house,
doesn't suck the life out you
A real love gives life
Makes you feel alive
Despite popular opinion
Love shouldn't make you feel weak
Make you feel like dying

or
Tell you that you're crazy
But if you are
Crazy
It lovingly refers you to a good psychiatrist

The Next One

I ain't listen to all of 444 cause' it put me in my feelings
Made me feel stupid
And less of a woman for picking the wrong
one more times than I needed
didn't know what love was
I'd never seen it
daddy showed loved by paying bills
for him that was an achievement
but his heart and the ways of men
he kept those secret
Leaving me open to those professing
love but didn't mean it
I couldn't read em
So, I believed em
Accepting their lies
and their semen
Hearts walled off
Like drywall
My tears couldn't reach em
My sex couldn't keep em
My energy made them strong and more appealing
To the next one

Always Remember

If
Love comes
Give into it
Completely
Be sure footed
As you jump
Off cliff
Don't fear being flattened by its weight
Give your whole heart freely
Wishing for nothing
In return
If you're able
Knock at its door
Confidently
Don't be furtive
For that helps no one and moves NoThing forward
And when the day comes -And it will
When you find yourself
Circling the floor, replaying arguments in your head, calling
yourself fool, and cursing the name one once cherished
Secure yourself
Stave off winter
Fight the temptation- to let bitterness settle
Know that
We've all
Felt the embrace and emptiness,
Nursed hearts broken too soon,
Looked for resolution in the bottom of empty glasses,
Left words hanging mid air
Been perpetrator
And victim
In love's courtroom

Who YOU Are

onlookers routinely catch me gazing
at the stars
call me crazy
not able to stretch me line straight
they hate me
moonwalker
sun child of dreams

tongue kissing ven-us
while you work 9-5
I fly 2 places unseen
by earth bound eyes
moonwalker
embodying ancestor dreams
I ski
hopscotch with stars
hide & go seek on Mars
we are one
you straddle sanity wide legged
and sweaty
I carelessly lick perspiration-
from my chin
daughter of the moon
mistress to the sun
draw me burning brightly
embracing my freedom

In Praise of The Wytch

Earth

We are the elements
Stay close to the ground
Omnipresent
Six feet under
Our mothers blood courses through our veins out our
wombs down our legs feeding hungry soil
We are dirty with your sadness
Different from anyone you know
Omnipotent
We lick wounds and swallow sorrows
Name ourselves Goddess
Are not afraid of the dark
Call on God, Angels & Ancestors when shit gets tight
We are round
Full figured
Full of ourselves

Water

We bathe in basil and sea salt
Were shackled but jumped ship anyway
Sharks fed on our flesh
We are ocean now
You eat us unknowingly
Drink us in
Believe you can suck us dry
And quiet our storms
But

We are Oya
Settling accounts
We are MA 'at
Shifting
You can't box us in, pin us down or tell our story

Fire

We eat men whole when given the chance
Burn
Sage
Incense
Candles
Tools of the trade
Dance under moons full
We are loud
Alive
Stretch things out to fit our shape
U Itch to see us put in our place
We are Witch, Wise Womyn and Crone
Burned at the stake

Air

We are immortal
Reincarnated in the poems of our daughters
We are phoenix
Eyes in the back of our head
We are sankofa bird
Live betwixt worlds, Float through walls that you build around us,
Blowing cigar smoke in your face, we are juke joint

Speak out both sides of our mouth; See your future in eggshells-it's not looking good for you
Familiars at our side we tag Miami, Haiti and Nawlins with chalk circles, drink with legba at the crossroads, Walk on water, Masquerade as poet, artist and mama
We
Eat too many carbs, fall in love with men who are afraid to love us back and turn our crooked noses up at your traditions
Jazz, poetry and Sade are our religions
We are
Black cat crossing your path, that poem you wish you smart enough to write,

The rhyme you are too afraid to spit, fucking up the mood we are the ejaculation that comes too quickly, Gas on a crowded elevator, the uninvited party guest flirting with your boyfriend and eating all your food

An inconvenient truth
We are the shoes you can't afford to buy, that thing you hate but can't let go,
Those pants that are too tight around your waist now, the song that keeps playing in your head, that chic you know you're not good enough to bang, the one your mama warned you about
We are trouble, urban sprawl haunting your daydreams

We are muse; inspire you to get your game up, teaching by example
We are Root Worker, Obeah Lady and Conjure Womyn, the scary broad living at the end of the road alone
Glamouring you through forked tongue we make miracles

And yes, mothafucka we DO Ride on Brooms
You should be afraid of Womyn like us
Chastity belted we fuck anyway
We do what we want to do
Walk butt naked in the daytime
And come to you at night
Carrying blessings, and justice in our left hand
Machete and curses in our right

Ancestor Message received December 2014
I AM constantly and perpetually busy about bringing heaven into earth. This is why we're here.

About the Author

Zoë Flowers is an author and international speaker whose poetry and essays can be found in several anthologies and journals. In 2004, Zoë interviewed survivors of domestic and sexual violence. ***From Ashes to Angel's Dust: A Journey Through Womanhood*** is the book that emerged from those stories. ASHES – is a play adapted from stories chronicled in the book and has had many successful performances including Yale University's Fearless Conference, The White House's United State of Women Summit in 2016, National Coalition against Domestic Violence's National Conference, Smith College, and Brown University.

Zoë has appeared on National Public Radio was the keynote speaker for The Florida Coalition Against Sexual Violence statewide conference, The New York State Coalition Against Domestic Violence, and The Maryland Women of Color Network's Conference in 2018. In 2019, she presented a workshop entitled, "Utilizing Performance as an Intersectional Response to Violence Against Women in Fez, Morocco and conducted listening sessions in London, UK and Edmonton, CA. She was also the keynote speaker at SUNY Adirondack's We. Say. No Conference, Delaware's Victim Service Conference, and returned as keynote for The New York State Coalition Against Domestic Violence Prevention Summit. In 2020, she taught several classes at the University of Florida, Loyola University and the University of Denver Colorado and provided virtual keynotes at The Victim Justice Symposium in Des Moines Iowa and the New Jersey Coalition Against Domestic Violence.

Printed in the United States
By Bookmasters